PRINCIPLES OF THE
FLUTE
RECORDER
& OBOE

Michel de La Barre and Other Musicians, painting ascribed to Robert Tournières. One of the seated wind players is presumed to be Jacques-Martin Hotteterre. (Reproduced by courtesy of the Trustees, The National Gallery, London.)

PRINCIPLES OF THE
FLUTE
RECORDER
& OBOE

(Principes de la Flûte)

JACQUES-MARTIN HOTTETERRE

Translated, with Introduction and Notes, by
PAUL MARSHALL DOUGLAS

Professor of Flute, Baroque Flute, Chamber Music,
Collegium Musicum, The University of British Columbia.
Founder and Director, The Vancouver Baroque Ensemble

DOVER PUBLICATIONS, INC., NEW YORK

Riverside Community College
SEP **'06** Library
4800 Magnolia Avenue
Riverside, CA 92506

This Dover edition, first published in 1983, is a new printing of
the work originally published by Dover in 1968 with the title
Rudiments of the Flute, Recorder and Oboe. The French work on
which this new translation was based was first published in Paris
in 1707 with the title *Principes de la Flute Traversiere, etc.*

Manufactured in the United States of America
Dover Publications, Inc., 31 East 2nd Street, Mineola, N.Y. 11501

Library of Congress Cataloging in Publication Data

Hotteterre, Jacques, 1674-1763.
  Principles of the flute, recorder, and oboe.

  Translation of: Principes de la flûte traversière.
  Previously published as: Rudiments of the flute, recorder & oboe.
  Bibliography: p.
  1. Flute—Methods—To 1800. 2. Recorder (Musical instrument)—
Methods—To 1800. 3. Oboe—Methods—To 1800. I. Douglas, Paul
(Paul M.) II. Title.
MT 342H7414 1983   788'.51'0712   83-20522
ISBN 0-486-24606-X

✠ *Contents* ✠

v

✗ *Translator's Introduction* ✗

It would indeed be difficult, if not impossible, to study the history of the development of the flute without considering one of its most significant milestones: The *Principes de la Flûte*[1] by Jacques-Martin Hotteterre.

The flute is one of the oldest, if not the oldest, of musical instruments. It has undergone many changes since its beginning and served many different purposes; and still, from antiquity to this day, it has maintained its high position in the world of music. Perhaps the most significant change occurred when the emphasis shifted from the recorder to the transverse flute at the turn of the eighteenth century.

The seventeenth century had seen in France a period of great artistic and cultural expansion and enlightenment. The Palais de Versailles had been constructed and Charles Le Brun appointed chief painter and artistic arbiter for Louis XIV. Racine had striven for, and achieved, simplicity, clarity and truth in his *Andromaque* and *Phèdre*, while Lully had graced the royal court with the charm and sophistication of his ballets and operas.[2]

The arts, promoted by Louis XIV during the *grand siècle*, had become indices of social stature. Persons wishing to achieve social prominence were expected to attain certain levels of

---

[1] *Principes de la Flute Traversiere, ou Flute d'Allemagne, de la Flute à Bec, ou Flute Douce, et du Haut-Bois, Divisez par Traitez.*

[2] A broader view of the artistic France of this period is given in: Paul Henry Lang, *Music in Western Civilization* (New York: W. W. Norton and Company, Inc., 1941), pp. 374–383.

proficiency in art, music and other intellectual fields. This drive for cultural and intellectual prestige brought about many changes in theoretical as well as practical concepts, among which was the search in music for clarity of form, conciseness and noble simplicity. This new movement was to reach its peak early in the eighteenth century in the works of François Couperin "Le Grand."

The enlightenment of the arts included specific developments in instrumental music. In the latter part of the seventeenth century, the orchestra had begun to crystallize into a definite form of five string sections. The harpsichord had come into its own. Of the wind instruments the oboe and the flute maintained their supremacy over all others. Many other varieties of instruments, naturally, still existed and were used, but gradually they gave way to their simpler, more popular relatives.

The direction of development was away from the more impersonal species in favor of instruments which offered increasing possibilities for individual expression. This trend, for instance, brought about, on the one hand, the downfall of the multi-stringed varieties of the string family, such as the hurdy-gurdies and violas d'amore, and on the other, the rise of the four-stringed violin family. It prevailed also over the wind instruments and resulted in the gradual dying out of the less personal types such as the bagpipes, or *musettes*, as they were known in France.[3]

Of the two flutes in use during the seventeenth century, the recorder had been the favorite. The transverse flute had been very much in use but had yet to find its place as an orchestral instrument. Until the second half of the century, the orchestra had not reached that point in its development where it required the power and tonal flexibility of the transverse flute, but, by the turn of the eighteenth century, with the development of the orchestra, the need for a more brilliant and expressive instrument superseded the prestige of the softer, less personal, recorder. The transverse flute offered, through the simplicity of

---

[3] Karl Geiringer, *Musical Instruments* (New York: Oxford University Press, 1945), pp. 114, 115.

its mouthpiece, possibilities of a wider range of tonal colors and dynamic expression.

These possibilities appealed greatly to orchestral flute players, who were constantly vying for supremacy with the oboists. For general orchestral purposes, the recorder simply did not satisfy the needs imposed by the new trends. As a solo instrument the brilliance of the transverse flute also gained the favor of flute enthusiasts, so that by the middle of the eighteenth century[4] the recorder saw only very limited use, and was, for all practical purposes, extinct.

Before this happened, however, the transverse flute as an orchestral instrument had been demonstrating its usefulness for some seventy-five years.

In the second half of the seventeenth century Lully's famous opera orchestra had risen rapidly in the esteem of the musical world of western Europe. It should therefore come as no great surprise that the transverse flute received invaluable impetus by its introduction into a Lully score in 1677.[5] This rapid rise in the popularity of the more brilliant instrument resulted in a definite need for an up-to-date instructional method for it. Hotteterre not only met this need, by writing his *Principes de la Flûte*, but provided also for those more conservative musicians who remained faithful to the recorder.

The Hotteterre name was famous in the second half of the seventeenth century and the first half of the eighteenth.[6] Through several generations members of this family enjoyed the reputation of master musicians and makers of musical instruments. Richard Shepherd Rockstro quotes J. A. Carlez as saying: "The Hotteterres were wind instrument makers who combined with their great skill as artisans talents no less great as instrumental performers. Their collective reputation should

4 H. M. Fitzgibbon, *The Story of the Flute* (London: The Walter Scott Publishing Co., Ltd., 1914), p. 20.
5 Geiringer, *op. cit.*, p. 140.
6 The family was so large that even the name varied quite extensively. Obterre, Otteterre, Hauterre, Hauteterre, Opterre, Haulteterre, Hautetère are some forms that are known. R. Cotte, "Hotteterre," *Die Musik in Geschichte und Gegenwart* (ed. Friedrich Blume, Kassel & Basel: Bärenreiter, 1949–), VI (1957), columns 783–788.

therefore have been doubly increased, but alas! in what estima-
tion were orchestral musicians, however skillful and deserving
they might have been, likely to have been held in the France
of Louis XIV? The mere fact the name of Hotteterre has survived may therefore be taken as sufficient proof of their
merits."[7]

To go into the details of the Hotteterre family would be beyond the scope of this introduction, especially since most
authorites do not agree upon the exact relationship of one member to another. Of singular significance is that one name has
survived more successfully than the others, that of Jacques-
Martin, called "le Romain." The only reason for this appella-
tion that the scholar Thoinan could find was that the young
Hotteterre is said to have made a trip to Italy during which he
spent some time in Rome; Thoinan adds, however, that this
theory has not been substantiated.[8]

Very little else is known with respect to Hotteterre's life. He
died, according to most authorities, in 1760 or 1761, his birth
date remaining to this day a matter of speculation. Despite
the lack of sure evidence, Roger Cotte holds that Jacques-Martin was born around 1680,[9] while De Lorenzo maintains that
"M. Jules Carlez (1877) has furnished almost positive proof
that he was born in Évreux, between the years 1640 and
1650."[10] These last dates are obviously erroneous when one
considers that, if the generally accepted date of his death is
correct, Hotteterre would have lived to the improbable age of
one hundred and ten to one hundred and twenty years.

Upon his return from Italy, (if he went), Hotteterre quickly
established himself as a master musician not only on the flute

---

[7] Richard Shepherd Rockstro, *The Flute* (London: Rudall, Carte and Co.,
1928), p. 534. Carlez's book, *Les Hotteterre*, was published by Le Blanc-
Hardel, Caen, 1877.

[8] "La raison qui valut au fils Hotteterre le surnom de Romain ne trouve
son explication, à défaut de preuves authentiques, que dans la probabilité
d'un voyage en Italie, entrepris par lui, et pendant lequel il aurait fait à
Rome un séjour plus ou moins prolongé." Ernest Thoinan [Antoine Ernest
Roquet], *Les Hotteterre et les Chédeville* (Paris: Sagot, 1894), p. 38.

[9] *MGG*, VI, column 783.

[10] Leonardo De Lorenzo, *My Complete Story of the Flute* (New York: The
Citadel Press, Inc., 1951), p. 65.

but also on other instruments. Along with other inheritors of the Hotteterre name, Jacques-Martin figured in many musical activities of the royal court. He was a member of the "douze grands hautbois et violons de la Grande-Écurie," a band of musicians who took part in all the royal ceremonials at which music was played.[11] In this group he played the bass oboe and the bass viol, positions in which he succeeded his kinsman, Jacques-Jean. In 1707 he received the title of "Ordinaire de la Musique du Roi," and shortly thereafter was named "Flûte de la Chambre du Roi."[12]

Hotteterre was known not only as a player, but also as a pedagogue and a composer. The esteem in which he was held as a teacher of wind instruments is indicated by the fact that he received better remuneration for his services than did the best organists of the time.[13] The instructional method, hereafter translated, is ample proof of his merits as a pedagogue in the field of instrumental music.

Jacques-Martin, often erroneously referred to as Louis,[14] derived his reputation only partly from his *Principes de la Flûte*. He is also known as the author of several other works relating to wind instruments, and the composer of many pieces for these instruments. Two other treatises appeared subsequently to the *Principes de la Flûte*. In the year 1712 he published *L'Art de Préluder sur la Flûte Traversière, sur la flûte à bec, sur le Haubois, et autres instruments de dessus* (published by Foucault and Hotteterre himself), and in 1738, *Méthode pour la Musette contenant des principes, par le moyen desquels on peut apprendre à jouer de cet instrument* (published by Christophe Ballard).

The only clue to the actual date of the first publication of the *Principes* is a date given on the frontispiece of the work, which represents a player of the transverse flute, presumably

---

11 De Lorenzo, p. 66.

12 According to Thoinan, *op. cit.*, pp. 38, 41.

13 "Les maîtres qui enseignaient à jouer de ces instruments—les Hotteterre, les Chédeville . . .—étaient mieux récompensés de leurs travaux que les meilleurs organistes." Michel Brenet [Marie Bobillier], *Les Concerts de France sous l'Ancien Régime* (Paris: Librairie Fischbacher, 1900), pp. 212–213.

14 Thoinan proves that this is an error; *op. cit.*, pp. 37, 38.

Jacques-Martin Hotteterre himself.[15] In some editions the date 1707 is printed next to the artist's name just below the lower left-hand corner of the figure on this frontispiece. Nevertheless Hugo Riemann states, for reasons known only to him, that Hotteterre "probably" wrote his *Principes* in 1699.[16] The original publisher of the *Principes* was Christophe Ballard.

Several different editions were examined during the course of this translation, but there seemed to be no difference between them. According to Dayton C. Miller, the English translation (172?) that exists in the Library of Congress in Washington, D.C., is a "unique work not found in any other library."[17] This early work was not used or consulted in any way during the course of this new translation.

The specific edition used for the present translation was the 1728 Amsterdam edition in French originally published by Étienne Roger. The work has recently been reprinted in facsimile with a German translation.[18]

The *Principes de la Flûte* contains a thorough explanation of the rudiments of playing the transverse flute, the recorder and the oboe, and includes detailed fingering and trill charts for these instruments. It also contains an important discussion on the principal ornaments and embellishments of the period. In this respect the work is a worthy companion to François Couperin's *The Art of Playing the Harpsichord* (1716). Until this time ornamentation had primarily been a matter of taste and tradition, but as the baroque period progressed and an increasing number of musical treatises appeared, it seemed only fitting that these embellishments be discussed within these treatises. This trend is further indicated by P. F. Tosi's *Observations on the Florid Song* (1723) and Quantz's *Essay on Flute Playing* (1752), both of which dwell extensively on ornamentation and the art of stylistic playing.

[15] Thoinan, *op. cit.*, p. 39.
[16] Hugo Riemann, "Hotteterre," *Encyclopaedic Dictionary of Music*, trans. J. S. Shedlock (Philadelphia: T. Presser, c. 1898), p. 360.
[17] Dayton C. Miller, *Catalogue of Books Relating to the Flute* (Cleveland: the author, 1935).
[18] Kassel & Basel: Bärenreiter, 1st ed. 1941, 2nd ed. 1958.

In his *Principes de la Flûte*, Hotteterre explains in great detail the correct way of playing such embellishments as trills, appoggiaturas, mordents and finger vibrati. With regard to these embellishments, it would be of interest to compare the treatises of Hotteterre, Couperin, Tosi and Quantz. As a text of performance practice of early eighteenth-century French music, Hotteterre's *Principes* has considerable practical value for the present-day student.

As a method for the recorder, the transverse flute and the oboe, the work also has considerable practical value. Since the recorder is practically the same today as it was at the turn of the eighteenth century, students wishing to learn to play this instrument will find in the treatise on the recorder a method of instruction as complete and concise as it is possible to find.

Because of the numerous and extensive transformations which the transverse flute and the oboe have undergone during the past two and a half centuries, the rudiments included in the treatises on these instruments obviously cannot apply to modern instruments. However, students and historians who have an active interest in ancient instruments and a desire to learn to play them will find these treatises extremely valuable with regard to the basic rules of playing the seven-hole transverse flute and oboe of Hotteterre's time.

❧ A Select Bibliography ❧

Baines, Anthony. WOODWIND INSTRUMENTS AND THEIR HISTORY. *New York: W. W. Norton and Co., Inc., revised ed., 1963.*

Blom, Eric, ed. GROVE'S DICTIONARY OF MUSIC AND MUSICIANS. *London: Macmillan and Co., Ltd., 5th ed., 1954.*

Blume, Friedrich, ed. DIE MUSIK IN GESCHICHTE UND GEGENWART. *Kassel & Basel: Bärenreiter, 1949–.*

Brenet, Michel [Bobillier, Marie]. DICTIONNAIRE DE LA MUSIQUE. *Paris: Librairie Armand Colin, 1926.*

————. LES CONCERTS DE FRANCE SOUS L'ANCIEN RÉGIME. *Paris: Librairie Fischbacher, 1900.*

Bukofzer, Manfred F. MUSIC IN THE BAROQUE ERA. *New York: W. W. Norton and Co., Inc., 1947.*

Carlez, J. A. LES HOTTETERRE. *Caen: Le Blanc-Hardel, 1877.*

Daubeny, Ulric. ORCHESTRAL WIND INSTRUMENTS ANCIENT AND MODERN. *London: W. Reeves, 1920.*

De Lorenzo, Leonardo. MY COMPLETE STORY OF THE FLUTE. *New York: The Citadel Press, Inc., 1951.*

Dufourcq, Norbert, ed. LAROUSSE DE LA MUSIQUE. *Paris: Librairie Larousse, 1957.*

Eitner, Robert. QUELLEN-LEXIKON DER MUSIKER UND MUSIKGELEHRTEN. *New York: Musurgia, 1947 (reprint).*

Fétis, F. J. BIOGRAPHIE UNIVERSELLE DES MUSICIENS. *Paris: Librairie de Firmin-Didot et Cie., 1883.*

Finney, Theodore M. A HISTORY OF MUSIC. *New York: Harcourt, Brace and Co., revised ed., 1947.*

Fitzgibbon, H. Macauley. THE STORY OF THE FLUTE. *London: The Walter Scott Publishing Co., Ltd., 1914.*

Geiringer, Karl. MUSICAL INSTRUMENTS. *New York: Oxford University Press, 1945.*

Lang, Paul Henry. MUSIC IN WESTERN CIVILIZATION. *New York: W. W. Norton and Co., Inc., 1941.*

Lavignac, Albert. ENCYCLOPÉDIE DE LA MUSIQUE ET DICTIONNAIRE DU CONSERVATOIRE. *Paris: Librairie Ch. Delagrave, 1913 et seq.*

Michel, François, ed. ENCYCLOPÉDIE DE LA MUSIQUE. *Paris: Fasquelle, 1958–1961.*

Miller, Dayton C. CATALOGUE OF BOOKS RELATING TO THE FLUTE. *Cleveland: the author, 1935.*

Riemann, Hugo. ENCYCLOPAEDIC DICTIONARY OF MUSIC. *Trans. J. S. Shedlock. Philadelphia: T. Presser, c. 1898.*

Rockstro, Richard Shepherd. THE FLUTE. *London: Rudall, Carte and Co., 1928.*

Sachs, Curt. OUR MUSICAL HERITAGE. *Englewood Cliffs, N. J.: Prentice-Hall, Inc., 2nd ed., 1955.*

———. THE HISTORY OF MUSICAL INSTRUMENTS. *New York: W. W. Norton and Co., Inc., 1940.*

Thoinan, Ernest [Roquet, Antoine Ernest]. LES HOTTETERRE ET LES CHÉDEVILLE. *Paris: Edmont Sagot, 1894.*

Welch, Christopher. SIX LECTURES ON THE RECORDER AND OTHER FLUTES IN RELATION TO LITERATURE. *London: Oxford University Press, 1911.*

PRINCIPLES OF THE
FLUTE
RECORDER
& OBOE

PRINCIPLES

OF THE

TRANSVERSE FLUTE

OR GERMAN FLUTE,

OF THE BEAKED FLUTE

OR RECORDER,

AND OF THE OBOE,

in Separate Treatises

By HOTTETERRE *le Romain, Musician-in-Ordinary to the King*

AMSTERDAM

Published by Estienne Roger, Bookseller,
who sells the most error-free Music in the World,
& who pledges to offer it at a lower price
than anyone else, even if he should
have to offer it for nothing.

PRINCIPES

DE LA

FLUTE TRAVERSIERE,

OU FLUTE D'ALLEMAGNE.

DE LA FLUTE A BEC,

OU FLUTE DOUCE,

ET DU HAUT-BOIS,

Divisez par Traitez.

Par le Sieur HOTTETERRE-*le Romain*, *ordinaire de la Musique du Roy.*

A AMSTERDAM,

Aux Dépens d'Estienne Roger, Marchand Libraire, qui vend la Musique du Monde la plus correcte, & qui s'engage de la donner à meilleur marché que qui que ce soit, quand même il devroit la donner pour rien.

℀ *Preface* ℀

Since the transverse flute is one of the most pleasant and popular of instruments, I feel a certain duty in undertaking this brief work to further the inclinations of those who aspire to play it. I also feel confident that my work will not be entirely unworthy of the curiosity of those who have a taste for this instrument, for my principal aim is to smooth out the first difficulties, which ordinarily cause the most grief. It is, therefore, possible to learn the principles of the transverse flute with the aid of this treatise. In it I give instructions on the manner of producing all the tones—naturals, sharps and flats—along with an explanation on how to perfect their intonation. I also indicate the method of playing trills on all these tones. Finally I indicate which ornaments are needed in order to play correctly and with taste. Without a teacher these rules and instructions could be sufficient for many people who have a natural aptitude for playing this instrument and who need only the fundamentals.

This work also includes a treatise on the recorder,[1] and a comparison between the transverse flute and the oboe which may serve as a method for learning to play the latter instrument. However, I do not discuss the note values or time. These matters are appropriate to a treatise on music rather than to one on the flute.

---

[1] In the original French, Hotteterre refers to the recorder as the "Flute à Bec ou Flute Douce." See: "Recorder," *Grove's Dictionary of Music and Musicians* (ed. Eric Blom, London: Macmillan and Co., Ltd:, 5th ed., 1954), VII, pp. 73-78.

TREATISE ON THE
TRANSVERSE
❧ FLUTE ❧

CHAPTER I

The Posture of the Body and the Position of the Hands

Since it is necessary, in order to reach perfection in the exercises in which one wishes to succeed, to combine as much as possible gracefulness and skill, I shall begin this treatise with an explanation of the posture one should assume while playing the transverse flute.

Whether one plays standing or seated, the body must be kept straight, the head high rather than low, turned slightly toward the left shoulder, the hands high without lifting either the elbows or the shoulders, the left wrist bent in and the left arm near the body. When in a standing position, one must be firmly fixed on one's legs, the left foot advanced, the body resting on the right hip, all without strain. One must, above all, refrain from making any body or head motions, as some do in beating time. When this posture is achieved, it is quite graceful, and will gratify the eye no less than the sound of the instrument will delight the ear.

With regard to the position of the hands, the demonstration found at the beginning of the treatise [i.e., the illustration facing this page] will be more instructive than all that I could write on this subject. One will learn from this figure that the left hand (A) must be placed in the higher position, the flute held between the thumb and the first finger (B), the wrist bent down, the fingers arranged in such a way that the first and the second are slightly curved and the third extended.

With respect to the right hand (C), the fingers must be held almost straight, the wrist bent down slightly, the thumb opposite the finger on the fourth hole, or a little lower, the little finger placed on the flute between the sixth hole and the molding of the key. All this can be seen demonstrated by the figure. The flute must be held almost level, slanting slightly toward the key (D).

CHAPTER II
The Embouchure [2]

Despite the fact that many people are convinced that embouchure technique cannot be taught by rules, there are some rules that greatly simplify the learning process. The advice of a good teacher, along with demonstrations, can spare those who seek this embouchure a great deal of trouble and difficulty.

I shall therefore provide both as much as it is possible to do so on paper. As for the demonstration, it can be seen in the figure at the beginning of this book [opposite page 9].

In regard to the teacher's advice, it will not be more difficult for me to write it than to deliver it orally; I shall do this as intelligibly as possible.

The demonstration shows the manner in which the lips are to be set. They must be joined, except in the middle where a little opening should be made to allow for an air passage. They should not be brought forward. On the contrary, they should be drawn back at the corners, so that they are smooth and straight. Place the mouthpiece against this little aperture, blow gently, press the flute against the lips and roll it constantly in and out until the true spot is found.

In order to observe all these rules, it will be of advantage to stand before a mirror. At first do not think of placing the

---

[2] In French *embouchure* bears a double meaning: (a) the formation of the lips necessary for tone production; (b) that part of the instrument which comes in contact with the mouth and by which tones are produced: the mouthpiece.

Since the French term *embouchure* has become generally accepted in the English language, we shall use it when referring to the first meaning.

fingers but only of blowing into the mouthpiece, trying to produce a sound. Then place the fingers of the upper hand, one by
one, and continue on each sound, blowing several times, until
it comes with assurance. After this, place the fingers of the
lower hand in the same order as those of the upper hand.
Beginners should not persevere too greatly in producing the
first pitch,[3] for which all holes are stopped, because it can be
produced only by stopping all the holes securely. This is more
difficult than it seems, unless one has had a little practice.

When the embouchure technique of the flute has been
grasped, it will be possible to begin the study of pitches. For
this the student will refer to Plate 1, the tones and semitones,
and will read the following chapter.

Furthermore, any rules which I have prescribed either for
the embouchure or for the position of the hands should be observed categorically only when the student does not find himself in a situation contrary to the one described above. For
example, if a person's lips were such that it would be more
difficult for him to produce the embouchure by smoothing and
straightening them than by extending the upper lip, he must
follow my rules only when they do not create an adverse situation, and he must always follow that which seems to be the
most natural.

In the same way, with regard to the hands, some players place
the upper hand in a position other than the one I have shown;
they hold out their wrist (arch-like) with the flute pressed
against the tip of the thumb. This hand position does not pre-
vent one from playing well, but it is neither as natural nor as
graceful. In addition, the flute is not as well fixed in place.
There are others who, because of not having had basic instructions, place the left hand below and the right hand above, and
hold the flute on the left. I shall not condemn this hand position altogether, since it is possible to play as well in this manner
as in another, and also because changing to another position
would present certain difficulties. However, those who have not
yet acquired these bad habits should beware of their pitfalls.

---

[3] The pitch referred to is the first one indicated on Plate 1: middle *D*.

CHAPTER III

First Explanation of Plate 1:
Natural Tones

Plate 1 serves two main purposes:

(1) The musical notes are shown on the five parallel lines, in the way seen at the top of the chart, and are distinguished by the names: Re, Mi, Fa, etc. and by *D, E, F*, etc. I have used both ways for the convenience of foreigners who would customarily use letters. The *G* clef,[4] which is seen on the second of the five lines, is the one most widely used for flute music. It gives its name to the second line, on which it is placed, and this position determines the names of the other notes according to the order that is followed in this demonstration.

(2) It contains a chart which explains how to finger each of the notes on the flute by stopping a varying number of holes. This chart consists of seven parallel lines, each corresponding to one of the seven holes on the flute.

On each one of these lines are a number of black or white zeroes [circles] which indicate whether the hole corresponding to each of these lines should be open or closed to produce a given tone. It is easy to understand that the black zeroes represent the holes that should be closed, and the white zeroes those that should be open. For instance, below the first note, which is *D*, there are seven black zeroes situated on the dotted

---

4 The original French reads: "La clef de *G. Ré, Sol*, ou de *Sol*, que l'on voit sur la seconde des cinq lignes. . . ." The meaning here is not clear, but it is apparent that Hotteterre refers to the common *G* clef.

All the Tones and Semitones of the Transverse Flute in Notation and with Fingering Chart

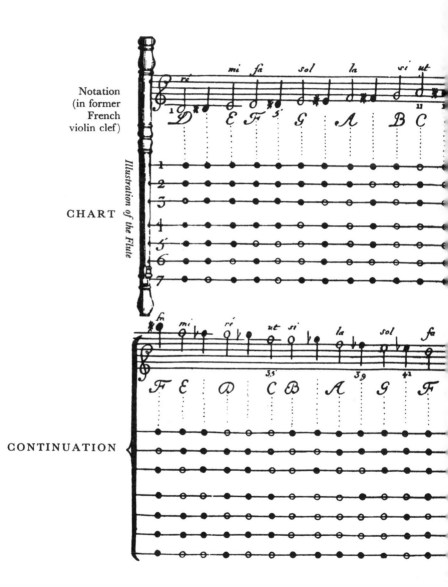

The lines above and below the five staff lines are added to fill out the entire range of the Flute.

perpendicular line. This indicates clearly that the seven holes of the flute are to be stopped, the first six by the fingers and the seventh naturally by the key. This produces the tone *D*. The student should proceed in this fashion for all the others, as I shall continue to explain more clearly.

With this plate the notes of the entire range of the flute can be studied, that is, all the natural tones as well as the sharps and flats. This range consists of two octaves and a few notes. The first octave extends from the first note to the thirteenth. The second octave extends from the thirteenth note to the twenty-fifth; it is produced in almost the same manner as the first with regard to fingering. The only difference is in the position of the lips, except for a few alterations in fingering certain notes, as is shown in the chart. I have indicated the naturals by white notes and the sharps and flats by black notes. This has been done for the benefit of those who have no knowledge of these principles.[5] These persons should not undertake anything too difficult at first; they should limit themselves to the naturals, without concern for the others until they have become a little more advanced. Remember that only a little air is needed to produce the low notes, and that all the holes indicated on the chart by black zeroes should be firmly stopped.

D   The pupil will then know how to produce the note *D*, by the seven black zeroes which are below it, as I have just explained.

E   Having made this tone, he will pass on to *E*-natural, the third note, which is produced by opening the sixth hole; this can be recognized by the open O, which I also call the white zero, located on the sixth line of the chart. Each note must be tongued. That is, the air stream must be articulated as if one were pronouncing quietly the syllable *tu*.[6]

F   *F* is produced by opening the fifth hole and stopping the sixth. This tone needs to be tuned by the embouchure. To

---

[5] The principles referred to are those involving the study of basic musical notation.

[6] The pronunciation of the French vowel *u* results in the proper lip and mouth formation for good tone production and articulation.

lower it, roll the flute inward. It is naturally a little high because the sharp is made on the same hole, as we shall see in the explanation of sharps and flats. It is necessary to remember to place the little finger between the sixth hole and the molding of the key, as I indicated in the second chapter.

G   *G* is produced by lifting all the fingers of the lower hand but leaving the little finger at the place I have just mentioned. This little finger must always remain here except when it is needed to activate the key. The pupil should quickly learn not to lift his fingers too high and to place them squarely on the holes.

As it was necessary to roll the flute inward for the *F*, it should be returned to its original spot for the *G*.

A   *A* is obtained by opening the third hole. The sixth finger must then be placed between the fifth and the sixth holes. This serves (as does the placement of the little finger) only to maintain the steadiness of the flute, but is important for the freedom of the fingers. As the pupil goes up the scale, he should little by little increase the intensity of the air.

B, C   *B* is produced by opening the second hole; *C*, by opening the first and stopping the second and third.

D   *D* is produced by stopping all the holes but the first. For this the blowing must be stronger to ensure a clear sound, while at the same time care must be taken not to overblow, for this would produce a sound one octave too high.

E   *E* is produced by opening the sixth hole, stopping the first and sustaining the air stream, as should be done for the ensuing tones.

F   *F* is produced by opening the fifth hole and stopping the sixth. Once again, on this note, the flute should be rolled inward.

G   *G* is produced by opening the fourth and the sixth holes without any other change. The flute should now be rolled back to its normal position. At this time permit me to point out to the beginners that as they rise in pitch on this instrument they

will find the embouchure progressively more difficult. Therefore to soften the high sounds and to produce them more easily
they should take pains to tighten their lips little by little, to
stretch them at the corners, to extend their tongue toward
their lips and to increase the intensity of the air.

A   *A* is produced by opening the third hole and sustaining the
air.

B   *B* is produced by opening the second hole.

C   *C* is produced by opening the first hole and stopping the
second, the fourth and the fifth. This tone is rather delicate
to tune, for there are some flutes on which it is high, and others
on which it is low. The means by which it can be lowered is to
soften it and to turn the flute inward. If this is not enough,
either the sixth hole should be stopped halfway without changing any of the others; or the demonstration on the chart should
be followed (thirty-fifth note). On the contrary, if the note is
found to be too low when played in the first manner described,
the third, fifth and sixth holes only should be stopped.

D   *D* is produced by stopping all the holes but the first. More
intense air is needed and the lips must be tightened.

E   *E* is produced by opening the third, fourth and seventh
holes and by stopping all the others. Note that the seventh hole
is opened by pressing the little finger on the key. Keep increasing the air.

Forced tones: All notes above *E* are forced tones and cannot
be used naturally in any piece. However, as it is not uncommon
to let a few of them slip into an improvisation,[7] I shall note
those that I have found. In any case, one must not insist on
producing them at the beginning. This is a great deal of trouble
the student would do well to spare himself until he is quite advanced. It would be well indeed, during the first days, not to
go beyond *G*, the eighteenth note, unless the embouchure
technique has been acquired with great ease. In this case the

---

[7] The French word *prélude* used here refers to the art of *préluder*, or improvisation. See: Michel Brenet [Marie Bobillier], *Dictionnaire de la Musique*
(Paris: Librairie Armand Colin, 1926), p. 367.

student could go up higher, but with discretion. Otherwise he would become frustrated without making progress, for it is absolutely necessary to begin by sounding the low tones well before going on to the others.

F   High *F* can almost never be played on the flute. I have, however, been able to do so on some instruments in the manner which I am about to explain, but one must not persevere in trying to produce it on all kinds of flutes, any more than the trills that derive from it, for this would be attempting the impossible. It is produced by stopping completely the first, second and fourth holes, by stopping the fifth only halfway, by opening the third, sixth and seventh holes and by blowing very strongly. In any case, I did not show it on Plate 1, because it is not at all a dependable note.

F♯   *F*-sharp is produced more easily, by stopping all the holes except the second.

G   *G* is produced by stopping the first and the third hole and by opening all the others.[7a] Notes higher than these can be obtained but they are forced to such a degree, and find such a limited use, that I advise no one to go to the trouble of trying to produce them.

[7a] Plate 1 shows the seventh hole closed. Here Hotteterre's diagram is more correct than his verbal description.

CHAPTER IV

First Explanation of Plate 2:
Trills on Natural Tones

🎼 🎼

After having gone through all the natural tones I shall discuss the trills, or shakes, which are played on these same tones. All examples are shown in the chart on Plate 2. I inserted at once all the tones and semitones, as I did in Plate 1, but to begin with I shall go through the trills only on natural tones, as I did for the regular tones. These will also be differentiated by white notes.

For the benefit of those who do not know what trills are, they can be described as an agitation of two sounds, either a step or a half step apart, which are played alternately in rapid succession. The trill is started on the higher note and finished on the lower. It is tongued only at the beginning, being continued only by the finger. The first trill on our chart—on low *D*—is produced by first opening the sixth hole, before even blowing, so as to start on *E*, which is the upper tone. The trill is played by tonguing the *E* and striking the sixth hole repeatedly, without stopping for breath or tonguing again. Finally the finger which produced the shake should come to rest on the same hole to finish the trill. The number of times the finger shakes is determined only by the value of the note. Remember, above all, not to rush the trill, but instead to delay it about half the value of the note, especially in the slow movements. This is shown in the trill chart. The shortest trill consists of three strokes, as on quarter notes in fast two-quarter and three-quarter time.

It would be superfluous to explain all the trills one after the other, because a quite clear chart is shown in Plate 2, and also because all the tones of which they consist should by now be known. The same rules apply to all these trills that applied to Plate 1 and all the same fingerings shown on the chart should also be observed.

I must single out only the C-natural trill, because it is really different from the others. It is begun by stopping all the holes but the first and shaking on the fourth after having sustained the appoggiatura.[8] It is finished by lifting the trill finger. This is the opposite of what should be observed with regard to the other trills. With respect to the trill on high C (twenty-third note), it is very difficult to play in tune and is actually very little used. Note that the D which precedes it on the chart is produced in an extraordinary way. The fourth and the fifth holes are trilled upon simultaneously and the sixth hole is slightly covered. Another way to play this trill is to shake on the third and sixth holes simultaneously while all others are stopped except the first. To finish the trill the active fingers must be raised. A vibrato[9] is often used on this note instead of a trill.

As soon as all the trills are learned on the natural tones, the pupil may try to play some simple, easy tunes, in order to become accustomed little by little to the sounds and to strengthen his embouchure. He can even go on to this exercise as soon as he has learned the natural tones of Plate 1. In this case he should refer to the trills of Plate 2 as he needs them. This will be less taxing to his memory. I shall give in Chapter Six another explanation of the trills.

[8] The French *port-de-voix* was an ascending appoggiatura. Hotteterre uses the term in this sense throughout this work with one exception: at the beginning of the trill the upper note is also designated as a *port-de-voix*. See: "Ornaments," *Grove's*, VI, p. 388.

[9] The French word *flattement*, as used here, refers to a type of finger vibrato which was used to embellish tones and add life and vibrancy to them. *Ibid.*, pp. 398, 399.

All the Trills or Shakes on the Transverse Flute

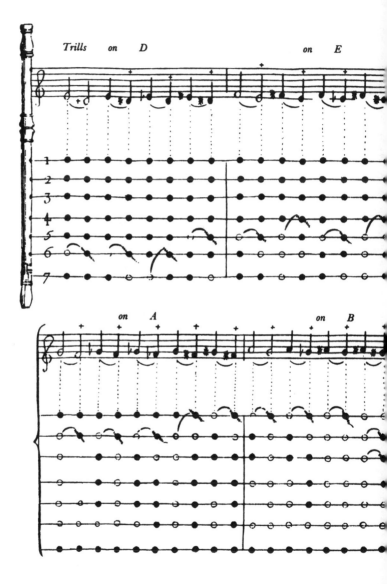

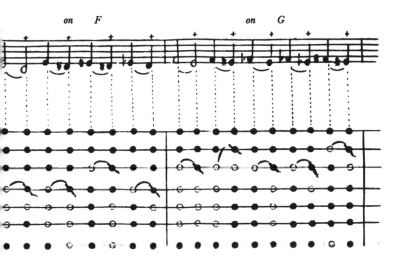

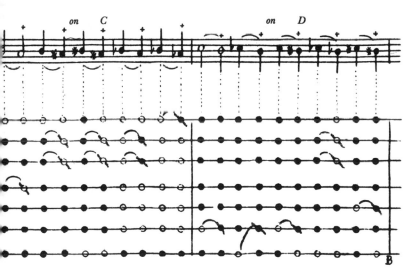

Plate 2a

Continuation of the Trills on the Transverse Flute

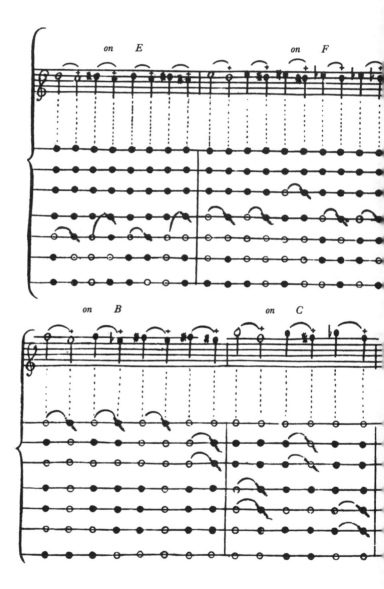

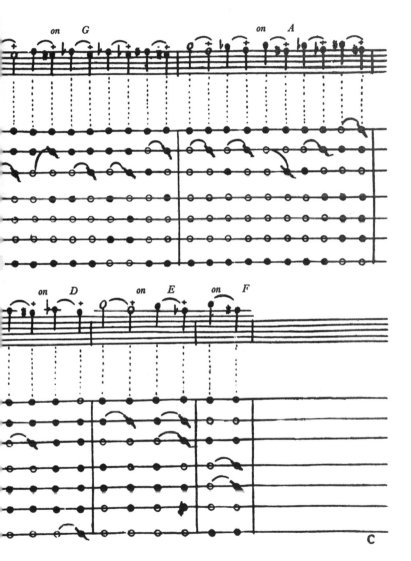

CHAPTER V

Second Explanation of Plate 1:
Sharps and Flats

As soon as the student has become well accustomed to the naturals, he can proceed to the sharps and flats. However, since there are several half steps that must be tuned by means of the embouchure, I shall explain them separately.

D One should start with D-natural (note one) so as to proceed with continuity from the naturals to the sharps and flats, and to accustom the ear as soon as possible to hearing the difference.

D♯ D-sharp is played next by pressing the little finger on the key to open the seventh hole.

E, F E and F will be played as I have indicated earlier in the explanation of natural tones. If one should ask me why there is no sharp between these notes, I shall answer that it is because there is but a half step from the one to the other.

E♯ For this reason, when E is sharped, F-natural is used. This produces the ordinary effect of the sharp, which is to raise the tone one half step. Remember to roll the flute inward. This is done by lowering the head slightly.

F♯ F-sharp is played by opening the sixth and seventh holes and leaving the fifth open as it already was. I am explaining in this manner so as to inform the student that he should not place his fingers on the holes after each note, and that he must lift them immediately according to the chart. To tune F-sharp

26

roll the flute outward and lift the head slightly. The expressions "roll the flute" and "roll the mouthpiece" bear the same meaning.

I shall no longer explain the fingerings, because I assume that by now the chart is well enough understood to render further explanations unnecessary. I shall discuss only the ways of correcting the intonation of the notes.

G, G♯ Since the flute was rolled outward for F-sharp, it must be rolled back to its regular spot for G, after which G-sharp is played and the flute is again rolled inward to tune it.

A, A♯ Roll it back to its original position for A-natural and inward for A-sharp. This note can be lowered still more by adding several fingers, as shown in the trill chart.

B, C Roll the flute back for B and C-natural. There is no sharp between these two notes for the same reason that I gave when speaking of E and F.

B♯ C-natural, therefore, will be used to play B-sharp.

C♯ To produce C-sharp the flute must be rolled outward as much as possible.

D, D♯ For D and D-sharp it should be in its normal position.

E, F E and F are subsequently played. There is but a half step between these two notes, as I noted when discussing the lower ones.

F♯, G, G♯ F-sharp, G-natural and G-sharp will be tuned in the manner explained earlier when discussing their counterparts an octave lower. I shall explain in Chapter Seven other ways of doing this but, this method being the easiest, it is best to learn it first.

A, A♯ For A-natural the flute should be in its normal position and rolled inward for A-sharp.

B, C, C♯ For B and C-natural it should be in its normal position and rolled outward for C-sharp. I shall explain this half step another way in Chapter Seven.

D, D♯ For D and D-sharp the flute should be rolled back to its normal position, unless they are too low, as they are on some flutes. In this case it must continue to be rolled outward. These high tones are difficult to play in tune; for this, one needs a good ear and practice.

E   The flute should also be rolled outward for *E*. More air is needed for this note.

As I explained high *F*-sharp and *G*-natural earlier, it would be superfluous to discuss them again here. Let us then proceed immediately to the flats, which are almost all related to the sharps, with this difference: the operation which flats one note, sharps the note below; this is because the flat lowers the tone a half step and the sharp raises it a half step. The trills are also all different, as can be seen on the trill chart. I shall not discuss the naturals further; nevertheless, it would be good to play them right along, as they are in Plate 1, and to correct their intonation, as I explained earlier.

E♭   We can then see by the chart that *E*-flat corresponds to *D*-sharp.

D♭   *D*-flat can also be played like *C*-sharp, but it is more in tune the way it is described on the chart.

B♭   *B*-flat is played like *A*-sharp. The flute must be rolled outward, which makes a certain difference between *B*-flat and *A*-sharp. On some flutes the seventh hole must be opened to ease the production of this tone.

A♭   *A*-flat is played like *G*-sharp.

G♭   *G*-flat can also be played like *F*-sharp, but it is more in tune the way it is described on the chart. To tune it the flute must be rolled inward to a great degree. This half step is very little used, and is encountered only in strongly chromatic keys, which are hardly ever used in composing for this instrument.

E♭   *E*-flat is played like *D*-sharp. The flute must be rolled outward.

D♭   *D*-flat is played like *C*-sharp. The flute must be rolled outward as much as possible for this tone.

B♭   *B*-flat is played like *A*-sharp.

A♭   *A*-flat is played like *G*-sharp. Do not roll the flute inward quite so much.

G♭   Like its counterpart an octave higher, this *G*-flat is different from *F*-sharp. It must also be tuned by rolling the flute inward. Many persons do not make this difference.

E♭   *E*-flat is played like *D*-sharp.

When I make a comparison between a flat and a sharp it is to be understood that it is between two adjacent notes. For example, I said that *E*-flat (penultimate note) is played like *D*-sharp (second note), and so forth for the others.

Any observations I may have made concerning the intonation of the half steps by rolling the flute inward or outward are fine points with which the student should not bother at the beginning, where the groundwork, so to speak, is but roughly laid out. He will, therefore, content himself with acquiring facility of embouchure and finger work. After achieving this, he can practice those refinements which are essential for perfection and which may be acquired only in time.

C♯   I did not explain low *C*-sharp in my chart, because this half step, artificially produced, has no particular fingering. It is played like *D* (note one), by stopping all the holes; the embouchure is turned in sufficiently to reach a half step. The trill is played as it would be on *D*.

CHAPTER VI

Second Explanation of Plate 2: Trills

To aid the understanding of signs located next to musical notes and on some of the circles on the chart of the second plate, I shall herewith give an explanation.

(1) The slur joining the two notes, indicated in Example 1, means that they should be tongued only once, on the first note, which acts as preparation, or appoggiatura, for the trill, and that they should be played continuously on one breath till the end of the trill. This I have explained earlier. The little cross before or over a note indicates that this is the note to be trilled.

EXAMPLE 1

(2) The line joining the two circles on the chart indicates the hole on which the trill starts and the one on which it ends. This, then, will indicate the borrowed trill fingerings, which are those that do not finish on the same hole on which the appoggiatura was done. For example, the *D* trill to *E*-flat starts on *E*-flat, by pressing the little finger on the key, and finishes on *E*-natural, by shaking the sixth finger on the sixth hole, and letting the key close and stop the seventh hole. There is also a wavy line on the second hole to indicate that it is on this hole that the finger should shake.

The trill from *E*-natural to *F*-sharp is of this nature. It is started by opening the fifth, sixth and seventh holes to play *F*-sharp, which acts as appoggiatura, and finished by restopping the fifth and shaking on the fourth. This widens the interval and brings out the trill more successfully than it would if the shake were on the fifth hole, which would not produce a sufficiently brilliant effect. Do not forget to release the key while trilling. This omission would sharpen the *E* and cause it to be out of tune. This is shown on the chart.

I shall also give an explanation of the difference between sharps and flats, by way of natural trills. For example, *E*-flat and *D*-sharp are produced in the same manner, but notice that the *E*-flat trill goes to *F*-natural and the *D*-sharp trill goes to *E*-natural. The first is a whole step while the other is a half step. This makes a notable difference. The situation is the same for all the other notes.

Notice also that trills and shakes are not always marked in pieces of music as I have described them here. The only mark is the little cross indicated in this manner: +. Nothing indicates the appoggiatura, but it must not be omitted. Everything I have explained above must be observed.

There are some high notes upon which it is not possible to trill. I discussed those that are possible, but it should be noted that those above high *B* (note twenty-two) are rarely used.

In addition, I did not discuss the means to correct the intonation of the trills. This would be only a repetition of what I have already explained concerning regular notes, of which these trills consist. I shall say only that a few of them must be started with the flute rolled inward, and finished with the flute rolled outward. Such is the trill from *F*-sharp to *G*-sharp, because these two notes need to be corrected differently. Other trills must be treated in the opposite way, as it becomes apparent from the explanation which I gave on all the notes in Chapters Three and Five.

With these explanations and the figures shown on Plate 2, it will be easy to learn to play all the trills. There are some which start by stopping the hole which is to be trilled and which end by opening this same hole. Such is the *C* trill (note eleven), of which I spoke in Chapter Four. This difference will become apparent by the disposition of the zeroes. In these cases the black zero precedes the white zero, contrary to the others.

CHAPTER VII

Comments on Certain Semitones and Trills

That nothing be omitted, I shall discuss here certain half steps and trills that can be obtained in a manner different from the way I have shown. I shall start with high G-sharp (note nineteen), although the way it is explained on the chart is the simplest. Nevertheless, it is a little high when played in this first manner, and there are several ways of lowering it.

(1) After having stopped the first, second and fourth holes (as is seen on the chart), the sixth hole is also stopped and the seventh is opened by means of the key. This method is fairly widely used; some performers even play the trills by shaking the fourth and sixth fingers simultaneously, but this is not too successful because it is difficult to produce a trill distinctly with two fingers so far apart. I would be in favor, then, of always borrowing the second-finger trill, as is shown on the trill chart, and of tuning it with the embouchure, by rolling the flute inward. Note that it is important not to lift the finger high in trilling.

(2) The first, second and fourth holes are stopped and the fifth only halfway, but with discretion. This method is a little less awkward than the other because only two fingers of the lower hand are used. These, being adjacent, will be more easily controlled. The trill always starts on the second finger, with the flute again rolled inward. There are certain passages where this half step should be played according to the chart, to avoid too great difficulty.

What I said about G-sharp applies also to A-flat (note

33

thirty-nine) except for the trill, which is different, as can be seen on the trill chart.

The high C-sharp trill (note twenty-four) can also be played in several different ways. I shall explain them and a few others here more to satisfy curiosity than to prescribe frequent use, because these trills cannot be obtained on all flutes with the same degree of ease.

The first way is to stop the second and third holes, and shake on the fourth and sixth simultaneously. All other holes must be open, even the seventh. In addition, the trill fingers must stop their holes in finishing the trill.

The second way is to stop all the holes except the first and the fifth. The trill is on the sixth hole, which is left open at the end of the trill. The key can also be trilled while observing the same conditions.

C-sharp without trill can also be played by stopping the third and fourth holes and leaving the others open. The same applies to D-flat.

I shall note, with regard again to high B-natural (note twenty-two), that it can be played by stopping the three holes of the lower hand and trilling as usual on the first hole. It is easily produced in this fashion, but it is a little too high. It is therefore necessary to roll the mouthpiece inward. The high B-flat trill (note thirty-seven) can be played by stopping the second hole only halfway and trilling on the first and third holes. It is also played by trilling on the first and third holes simultaneously, leaving all the others open, but it is not pure this way.

The A-sharp trill (note twenty-one) can be played by stopping all the holes except the third and the seventh, by trilling on the second hole and rolling the mouthpiece inward.

The high D-natural trill (note twenty-five), started on E-flat, can also be done on the fifth and sixth holes simultaneously, while stopping the first three, opening the fourth and the seventh, blowing hard and leaving the trill fingers in a raised position when finishing the trill. On some flutes it is necessary to open the first hole.

I shall mention, with regard again to low *C*-natural (note eleven on Plate 1), that some performers play it by stopping the second, fourth and fifth holes, but to me this method does not seem satisfactory, because in playing it in this manner it is too close to *C*-sharp, and the half step is not in tune.

CHAPTER VIII

Tonguing, Appoggiaturas, Springers,[10] and Terminated Trills on the Transverse Flute and Other Wind Instruments

After having explained the manner of playing tones and semitones with all their trills, there still remain to be discussed tonguing and ornamentation, which are absolutely necessary for perfect performance. These ornaments consist of appoggiaturas, springers, terminated trills, vibrati, mordents,[11] etc. I shall begin with all tonguings, articulations and slurs, of which I shall give several examples, as I shall for the appoggiaturas, springers, and terminated trills. These will be useful for all wind instruments. Then I shall explain the way to produce vibrati and mordents on the transverse flute.

To make playing more pleasant, and to avoid too much uniformity in tonguing, articulation is varied in several ways. For example, two main tongue strokes are used: *tu* and *ru*.[12] The *tu* is the more common, and is used almost everywhere, as on whole notes, half notes, quarter notes, and on most eighth notes, for when these last are on one line, or when they skip, they are tongued with *tu*. When they ascend or descend in a stepwise fashion, *tu* is also used, but it is alternated with *ru*, as is

---

10 The French text has *Accents*; *ibid.*, p. 418.

11 The French text has *Battements*; *ibid.*, p. 410.

12 The use of this word as a tonguing device presupposes that the *r* is not uvular but alveolar. This would produce the effect of a soft *d*-sound, which is closer to the tonguing characteristics desired, especially when used alternately with *tu*.

seen in Examples 2 and 3, where these two tonguings are alternated.

Note that the *tu, ru* is governed by the number of eighth notes. When the number is odd, use *tu, ru* immediately as in

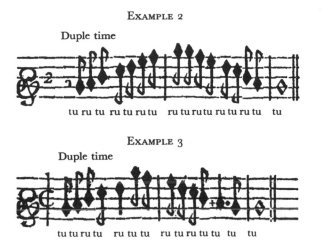

EXAMPLE 2

Duple time

tu ru tu   ru tu ru tu   ru tu ru tu ru tu ru tu   tu

EXAMPLE 3

Duple time

tu tu ru tu   ru tu tu   ru tu ru tu tu tu   tu

Example 2. When it is even use *tu* on the first two notes, and then *ru* alternately, as in Example 3.

It is well to note that all eighth notes should not always be played equally, but that in some time signatures one long and one short should be used. This usage is also governed by the number. When it is even, the first is long and the second is short, and so on for the others. When it is odd, the opposite is done. This is called dotting. The times in which this method is ordinarily used are two-four, simple three and six-four.

Ru should be used on the note following the eighth note when it ascends or descends in a stepwise fashion (Examples 4 and 5).

EXAMPLE 4

Three-four time

tu tu ru   tu   tu tu ru   tu tu ru   tu

EXAMPLE 5

Six-four time

tu ru tu tu ru tu tu tu tu

There are also some movements for which only *tu* is used for the eighth notes (Examples 6, 7 and 8).

EXAMPLE 6

tu   tu tu tu tu   tu tu   tu tu ru   tu

EXAMPLE 7

tu   tu   tu tu   tu   tu tu   tu tu tu ru tu   tu

EXAMPLE 8

tu   tu   tu tu   tu   tu tu tu   tu   tu tu ru tu

ru tu ru tu   tu

Tu is used on all these eighth notes and *ru* is used only on the sixteenth notes. The eighth notes are conceived as quarter notes and the sixteenth notes as eighth notes in this type of movement, as well as in six-eight, twelve-eight and nine-eight time. Also, in these times, the eighth notes must be played evenly and the sixteenth notes dotted.

Ru is used on sixteenth notes according to the rules given for eighth notes. It is even more frequently used here, because whether these sixteenth notes are on one line or skip, it is still used without fail (Examples 9, 10 and 11).

EXAMPLE 9

tu tu ru   tu tu tu tu   tu

EXAMPLE 10

tu tu ru tu tu tu tu ru tu tu tu ru tu   tu

EXAMPLE 11

tu tu ru   tu ru tu ru tu ru tu ru   tu

Although these rules are general, they admit exceptions in some passages, as can be seen in Examples 12 through 15.

EXAMPLE 12

tu tu ru tu   tu tu ru tu ru   tu

EXAMPLE 13

tu   ru   tu tu tu ru   tu   tu

EXAMPLE 14

tu tu ru   tu   tu ru tu tu ru   tu

EXAMPLE 15

tu tu tu ru tu tu ru tu tu ru tu tu ru tu tu ru tu

It is understood that *tu, ru* is used for the first two eighth or
sixteenth notes in even numbers, and this occurs frequently

when two eighth notes are intermingled with quarter notes, or sixteenth notes with eighth notes. It is done to achieve more softness and is a matter of taste. This taste, then, must be a guide if the tonguing becomes harsh when produced according to the manner which I prescribed in the first examples. The performer must stop when he reaches that point which seems to be the most pleasing to the ear, without concern for the arrangement of the notes or the different movements. Note only that *ru* must not be used on trills, or two consecutive notes, because it must always be used alternately with *tu*.

In three-two time *tu*, *ru* is used on the quarter notes, and *ru* on the half notes following a quarter note, ascending or descending in a stepwise manner (Example 16).

EXAMPLE 16

It is possible then to state that all triple meters are related to simple three-four time, and that in three-two time half notes are considered as quarter notes, and quarter notes as eighth notes. It is for this reason that the quarter notes must be dotted, in this time, according to the explanation which I gave earlier concerning eighth notes.

It should be noted that the tonguing may be more or less sharp, depending on the instrument. For example, it is soft on the transverse flute, sharper on the recorder and very pronounced on the oboe.

SLURS

Mention should be made of slurs. These consist of two or more notes played on one stroke of the tongue, and are indicated above or below the notes by ties (Examples 17 and 18).

EXAMPLE 17

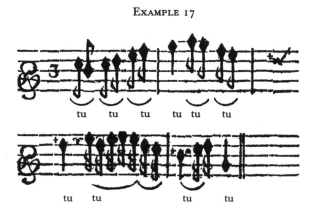

EXAMPLE 18

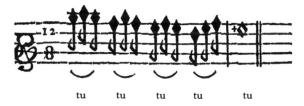

APPOGGIATURAS AND DESCENDING PASSING TONES[13]

The ascending appoggiatura is a stroke of the tongue anticipated by a step below the note upon which it is to be played (Example 19). The descending appoggiatura is started one step above and is hardly ever used except in descending thirds (Example 20).

---

13 The French title of this section is *Du Port-de-voix, & du Coulement.*

EXAMPLE 19

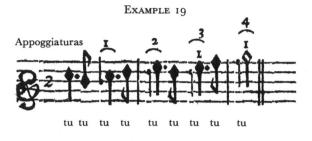

Appoggiaturas

tu tu   tu   tu   tu   tu   tu   tu   tu

EXAMPLE 20

Descending passing tones

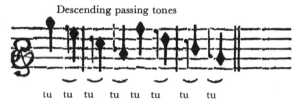

tu   tu   tu   tu   tu   tu   tu   tu

The little notes which indicate the lower and upper suspensions are not counted in the timing. They are nevertheless tongued, while the main notes are slurred. Mordents and ascending appoggiaturas are often linked, as can be seen in the example of the ascending appoggiaturas marked 3 and 4 in Example 19. Mordents will be learned in Chapter Nine.

SPRINGERS AND TERMINATED TRILLS

The springer is the sound attached to the end of certain notes to give them more expression (Example 21). The terminated

EXAMPLE 21

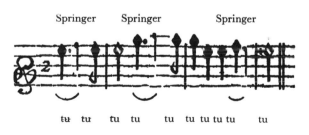

Springer   Springer   Springer

tu   tu   tu   tu   tu   tu tu tu tu   tu

trill is an ordinary trill followed by two sixteenth notes, slurred or tongued (Example 22).

EXAMPLE 22

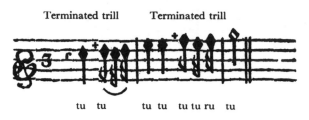

Terminated trill   Terminated trill

tu   tu   tu tu   tu tu ru   tu

CHAPTER IX

Vibrati and Mordents

Vibrati are produced almost like the regular trill, with this difference that the finger is always raised at the end, except on *D*. In addition, it is done on holes which are further away, and some on the edge of holes. Contrary to the trill, it involves the lower note.

The mordent is played by rapidly striking the hole once or twice, stopping it, as close as possible to the note that is to be played. Again, the finger must be raised at the end, except on *D*, as I shall explain presently. The mordent also involves the lower tone.

Following the order of Plate 1, I shall start with the vibrato on low *D*-natural, which can be produced only artificially. As no finger can be used to produce this ornament (since they are all in use stopping the holes), the lower hand shakes the flute in an effort to imitate the ordinary vibrato. As for the mordent, it is unobtainable.

The *D*-sharp, or *E*-flat, vibrato is played like that of *D*-natural. The mordent is played by the little finger on the key, upon which it must remain.

The *E*-natural vibrato is played on the edge of the sixth hole. The mordent is played on the hole itself.

The vibrato and the mordent on *F*-natural and *F*-sharp are played on the fifth hole; the vibrato is played on the edge of the hole, and the mordent on the hole itself.

The *G*-natural vibrato can be played two ways: on the edge of the fourth hole or on the fifth hole. The mordent is played on the fourth hole itself.

The vibrato on *G*-sharp, or *A*-flat, is played on the edge of the third hole, the mordent on the hole itself.

The *A*-natural vibrato is played on the fourth hole or the edge of the third, the mordent on the third itself.

The vibrato on *A*-sharp, or *B*-flat, is played on the sixth hole, the mordent on the same hole, or on the second when it is preceded by an appoggiatura.

The *B*-natural vibrato is played on the third hole, the mordent on the second.

The *C*-natural vibrato is played on the fourth hole, the mordent on the fourth and fifth holes simultaneously, or on the first when it is preceded by an appoggiatura.

The *C*-sharp, or *D*-flat, vibrato is played on the second hole, the mordent on the first.

The *D*-natural vibrato is played on the second hole. It is different from the others in that both at the beginning and at the end the hole must be stopped. Remember not to lift the finger too high. The mordent is played on the fourth hole when *C*-natural is used, and on the second and third holes simultaneously when *C*-sharp is used. Again the holes must be stopped at the beginning and at the end.

The *D*-sharp, or *E*-flat, vibrato is played on the first hole, which must be stopped at the beginning and at the end. The mordent is played on the key for *E*-flat, as I explained for the lower *E*-flat. *D*-sharp is played on the second and third holes simultaneously. In finishing this mordent the first hole must be opened, and the second and third stopped.

The vibrati and mordents from this tone on, to the *A*-sharp, or *B*-flat, are played like their counterparts an octave lower. The vibrato of this last note is played on the edge of the fourth hole. The mordent can be played on this hole or else on the second, especially when it is preceded by an appoggiatura.

The *C*-natural vibrato is played in two ways, either on the sixth hole or on the third. The mordent is played in the same manner, but also on the first hole when it is preceded by an appoggiatura.

The *D*-natural vibrato is played on the second hole, as is its counterpart an octave lower. The mordent is played on the second and third holes simultaneously.

The vibrato of *D*-sharp, or *E*-flat, is played the same as an octave lower; the mordent is played in the same manner, or else on the fifth and sixth holes simultaneously. The fourth and seventh holes must remain open. At the end all the fingers must be down.

The *E*-natural vibrato is played on the edge of the third hole, the mordent on the hole itself.

I shall omit the higher notes because they are too strenuous. The student should not even play some of these last notes until he is quite advanced.

These ornaments are not indicated in all pieces of music, and are ordinarily found only in those written by teachers for their pupils, in the manner shown in Example 23.

EXAMPLE 23

Vibrato   Mordent

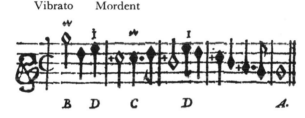

B   D   C   D   A.

In general, it would be difficult to give precise instructions as to where these ornaments should be placed in playing. On the whole it can be said that vibrati are frequently introduced on long notes: as on whole notes (A in Example 23), on half notes (B), on dotted quarter notes (C), etc. The mordents are ordinarily played on short notes: as on plain quarter notes (D) in fast movements, and on eighth notes in the time signatures in which these are played evenly. It is hardly possible to give more positive rules concerning the distribution of these ornaments. Taste and experience, rather than theory, teach their proper use. I would advise that the student first play pieces in which all ornaments are indicated, in order to become accustomed gradually to their execution on the notes where they will be most successful.

End of the Treatise on the Transverse Flute.

TREATISE ON THE
🌿 RECORDER 🌿

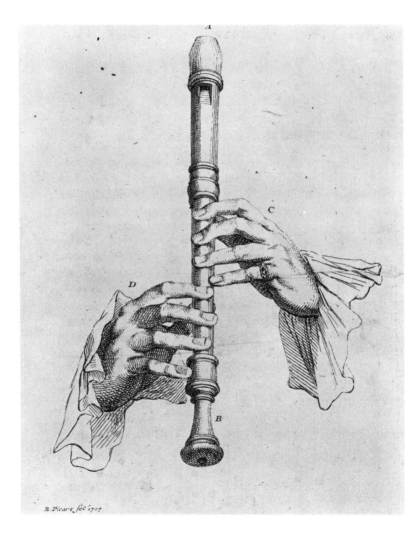

B. Picart fec 1707

CHAPTER I

The Position of the Recorder and the Position of the Hands

🎼 🎼

Since the recorder possesses its own merits and advocates, as does the transverse flute, I thought it not altogether useless to offer a short treatise concerning this instrument in particular.

I shall begin by an explanation of the manner in which the recorder should be held and of the position of the hands. This can be seen in the figure on the opposite page.

(1) The player must hold the recorder straight in front of him, put the upper end (A), called the beak, up to his lips without allowing it to intrude between them. The lower end (B), called the foot, should be held about a foot away from his body, in such a way that his hands may be placed on top of the recorder without strain. He should not elevate his elbows, but should let them fall free next to his body.

The left hand (C) should be placed on the upper half of the recorder and the right hand (D) on the lower half, as is shown in the figure. The left thumb stops the hole on the under side of the recorder. This hole is the highest and shall be called the first hole. The next one down I shall call the second, and so forth on down. The right thumb should also be placed on the under side of the recorder, opposite the finger on the fifth hole, or even a little lower. This thumb has no function other than that of supporting the instrument.

The fingers should be held as straight as possible, especially those of the lower hand. The little finger of the right hand should become accustomed to stopping the eighth hole. This is a little difficult at the beginning. The holes should not be stopped with the fingertips but with the middle of the top joint.[14] Since the middle finger on each hand is longer than the others, it should be bent slightly. This will cause it to fall more securely on the hole, stopping it more easily.

---

[14] Literally: "with the end of the finger passing the hole by about three or four *lignes*." The French *ligne* measures one eleventh of an inch. See also footnote 16, page 71.

CHAPTER II

Explanation of Plate 3: All the Tones

Since the chart that I shall use in the treatise is similar to that which was used in the treatise on the transverse flute, it would be superfluous to offer a second explanation here. Persons, then, who wish to begin with the recorder should study Chapter Three of the aforementioned treatise. They will be able to learn sufficiently about this chart as well as about the notes of music. It will nevertheless be necessary to change a few items in that chapter to make it completely applicable to Plate 3 on tones and semitones on the recorder. For example, there are eight holes on the recorder whereas there are but seven on the transverse flute. The first note on the recorder is *F* whereas on the transverse flute it is *D*. These distinctions then should be made and the passage on page 13, lines 13–14, should be read: "This chart consists of eight parallel lines, each corresponding to one of the eight holes on the recorder," while the passage beginning six lines lower should be read: "below the first note, which is *F*, there are eight black zeroes situated on the dotted perpendicular line. This indicates clearly that the eight holes of the recorder are to be stopped, the first four by the upper hand, and the remaining four by the lower hand. This produces the tone *F*."

The rest is the same except for page 16, line 12, where the following change should be made. "The only difference is in the embouchure."

Chapter Three can be followed up to page 16, line 22, where the explanation of the notes begins. Here we shall leave that chapter and resume the present one.

53

All the Tones and Semitones of the Recorder in Notation and with Fingering Chart

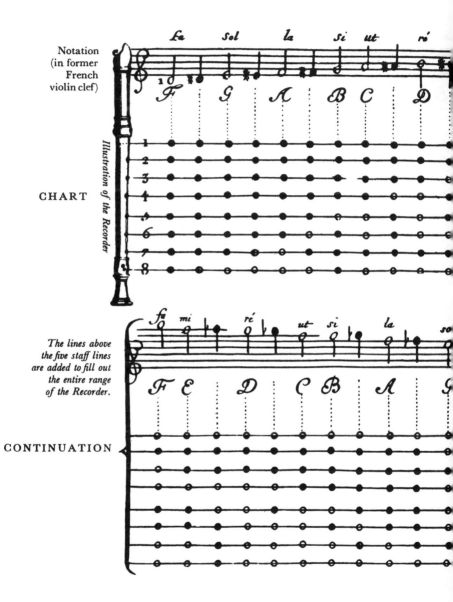

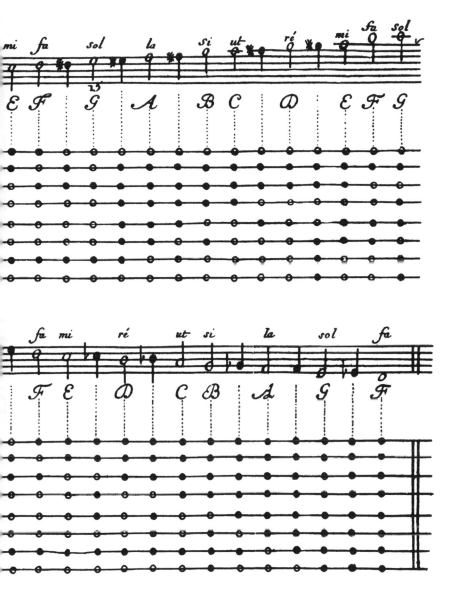

F The chart of Plate 3 shows that for *F* all the holes must be stopped. This note must be tongued, as I pointed out in Chapter Three of the treatise on the transverse flute. The problem here is to stop all eight holes firmly, because if there is the slightest leakage of air, this note cannot be produced. This difficulty stems partly from the fact that at first the little finger, which must stop the eighth hole, is not easily separated from the others. It is better, then, to start with *G*. This method will be more meaningful, and also is more commonly used. Nevertheless, to follow things in order, I shall discuss *F*-sharp.

F♯ It is produced by opening half of the eighth hole on those recorders which do not have the double eighth hole. On those which do have it only the farther hole is to be opened. This is done by sliding the finger back without lifting it. Remember to blow very gently on the lower tones, and gradually harder as the higher notes are played.

G *G*-natural is produced by opening the eighth hole fully.

G♯ *G*-sharp is produced by opening the seventh hole only halfway, in the manner which I explained concerning *F*-sharp. If the hole is double, only the farther aperture should be opened.

A *A*-natural is produced by opening the seventh hole fully, without restopping the eighth hole.

A♯ *A*-sharp is produced by opening the sixth hole and restopping the seventh.

B *B*-natural is produced by opening the fifth hole and stopping all the others.

C, B♯ *C*-natural is produced by opening the sixth and eighth holes and leaving the seventh stopped. This hole is almost always stopped, as shown on the chart. There is no sharp between *B* and *C*, the reason being that there is but a half step between these two notes. This is why *C*-natural is used to play *B*-sharp.

C♯ *C*-sharp is produced by opening the fourth hole and stopping the fifth and sixth.

D *D*-natural is produced by opening the fifth and sixth holes, with no other change.

D♯ *D*-sharp is produced by opening the third hole and stopping the fourth and fifth.

E *E*-natural is produced by opening the fourth and fifth with no other change.

F, E♯ *F*-natural is produced by opening the second hole and stopping the third hole. This hole is almost always stopped. There is no sharp between *E* and *F* for the same reason that I gave with regard to *B* and *C*. *F*-natural is therefore used to play *E*-sharp.

F♯ *F*-sharp is produced by opening the first hole, otherwise known as the thumb hole, and stopping the second hole.

G *G*-natural is produced by opening the second hole with no other change.

G♯ *G*-sharp is produced by stopping all the holes except the first and the eighth.

A *A*-natural is produced by opening the seventh hole with no other change. Here the blowing must be stronger to produce the higher tones of the recorder. This note is also produced by pinching.[15]

Pinched tones. This is done by stopping the thumb hole halfway with the thumbnail. This is done for all the high notes, as is shown on the chart by half-closed zeroes.

A♯ *A*-sharp is produced by opening the sixth hole and stopping the seventh only halfway. Pinching is required for this note as well as for all ensuing notes.

B *B*-natural is produced by opening the fifth and seventh holes and stopping the sixth.

C *C*-natural is produced by opening the sixth hole. This means that all the fingers of the lower hand are raised.

C♯ *C*-sharp is produced by opening the fourth hole, by stopping the fifth and by blowing a little more gently. Some

---

15 See: Christopher Welch, *Six Lectures on the Recorder and Other Flutes in Relation to Literature* (London: Oxford University Press, 1911), pp. 58, 122.

flutes have a double fourth hole. In such cases the fourth hole is opened only halfway and the fifth is not stopped at all.

D *D*-natural is produced by opening the fourth hole and raising all the fingers of the lower hand.

D♯ *D*-sharp is produced by stopping the sixth, seventh and eighth holes, with no other changes. On some flutes the eighth hole can remain open.

E *E*-natural is produced by opening the seventh and eighth holes and by stopping the fifth and sixth with no changes to the upper hand.

F *F*-natural is produced by opening the third hole, with no other change. There is no high *F*-sharp.

G *G*-natural is produced by opening the third and sixth holes and stopping all the others. It is necessary to blow very hard.

When all these notes have been studied, I shall assume that the chart is understood well enough to study the remaining notes, the flats. This will be all the easier because they are all related to the sharps, in that the operation which flats one note sharps another, as is shown on the chart. This was explained in Chapter Five of the treatise on the transverse flute. I shall therefore give no further explanation except for low *E*-sharp, which was not shown on the chart.

E♯ It is just the same as *F*-natural, as I explained for the higher *E*-sharp.

I should like to warn beginners against being too concerned at first with notes other than the naturals, which are indicated by white notes. They will thus avoid a great deal of difficulty.

CHAPTER III

Explanation of Trills

After learning all the natural tones, the student should learn to play the trills on these notes. For this he should study Chapters Four and Five of the treatise on the transverse flute. Here he will find a thorough explanation of trills, which he will use to learn those for the recorder. These are shown on Plate 4. I shall, therefore, discuss only a few particular trills, which will be enough to understand all of them. I shall begin with the low *F* trill, the first one on the chart. This chart shows the eighth hole open at the beginning of the trill and closed at the end. In the treatise on the transverse flute it was learned that the finger must strike several times the hole upon which the trill is to end. The same rule must be carried out for all the other trills.

F-sharp is trilled like *F*-natural, except that the finger falls on only half of the hole. If the hole is double the trill is played only on the nearest aperture, sliding the finger away.

The trill from *F*-sharp to *G*-sharp is played by first opening half of the seventh hole, by stopping half the eighth hole, with no further change, and by trilling on the seventh hole, stopping it entirely. These three moves are done consecutively and are preceded by a single stroke of the tongue. This trill is very little used.

The trill from *F* to *G*-flat is played by first opening half of the eighth hole and trilling on this same hole, stopping it entirely. This trill is used also for *E*-sharp.

The explanation of these four trills, in addition to the chart, should be enough to understand fully all the others. I shall men-

59

All the Trills or Shakes on the Recorder

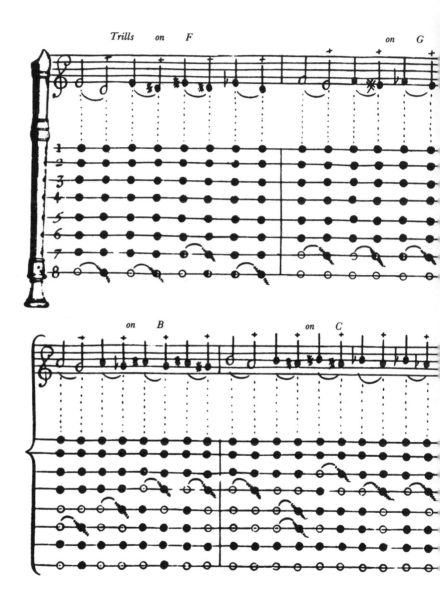

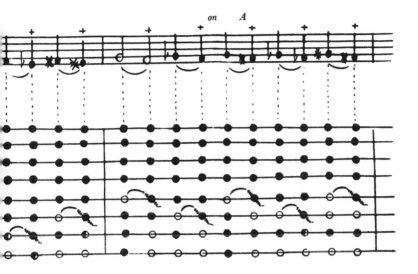

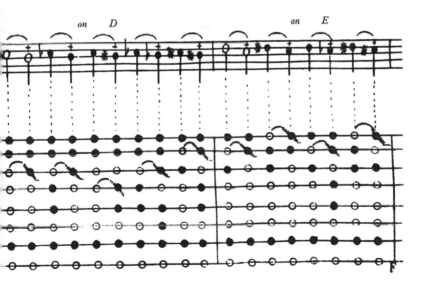

Continuation of the Trills or Shakes on the Recorder

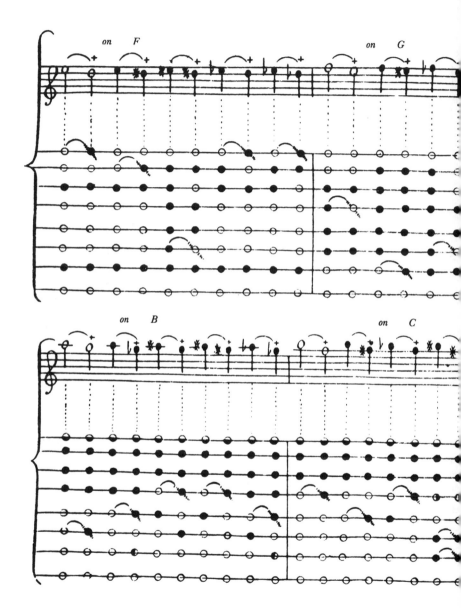

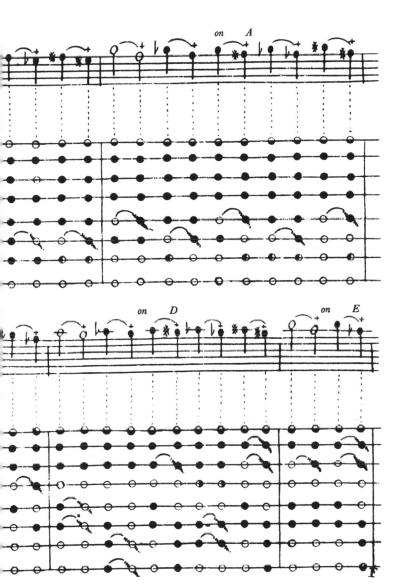

tion only the *G*-natural trill in the first octave (note fifteen) because it is played in a manner different from the others. This trill is started on *A* by stopping only the third, fourth, fifth and sixth holes and striking the fourth hole, which must remain open at the end. This is shown by the wavy line drawn through the open zero. There are still other trills similar to this one and also some which are played with two fingers simultaneously. This is shown on the chart by two wavy lines drawn through two zeroes, the one above the other.

There remains only to discuss vibrati and mordents, which will be explained in the next chapter. With regard to tonguings, slurs, appoggiaturas, springers etc., the student should read Chapter Eight of the treatise on the transverse flute, in which a thorough explanation is given.

CHAPTER IV

Vibrati and Mordents

In Chapter Nine of the treatise on the transverse flute I described vibrati and mordents and the manner in which they should be produced. The student should, therefore, read the beginning of that chapter before reading this one. Then he should study the following explanations on the manner of applying these rules to the recorder.

In keeping with the order of Plate 3 we shall start with the *F* vibrato. This can be played only by shaking the recorder with the lower hand, in the same manner that I explained for the first tone of the transverse flute. The same holds true for the *F*-sharp and the *G*-flat. No mordents can be played on these tones.

The *G*-natural, *G*-sharp and *A*-flat vibrati are played on the edge of the eighth hole, their mordents on the hole itself.

The *A*-natural vibrato is played on the edge of the seventh hole, the mordent on the hole itself.

The *A*-sharp, or *B*-flat, vibrato is played on the edge of the sixth hole; it can also be played on the eighth hole. The mordent is played on the sixth hole itself.

The *B*-natural vibrato is played on the edge of the fifth hole, the mordent on the hole itself.

The *C*-natural vibrato is played either on half of the fifth or half of the sixth hole. The mordent is played on the sixth hole itself except when the *B* is flatted. In this case the mordent is played on the fifth hole.

The C-sharp, or D-flat, vibrato is played on the edge of the fourth hole, the mordent on the hole itself.

The D-natural vibrato is played on the fifth hole, the mordent on the fourth, except when it is preceded by a half-step appoggiatura. In this case the mordent is played on the fifth and sixth.

The D-sharp, or E-flat, vibrato is played on half of the sixth hole. The mordent is played on the sixth hole itself, or on the third when it is preceded by an appoggiatura.

The E-natural vibrato is played on the fourth hole. The mordent is played on the third, or on the fourth when it is preceded by a D-sharp.

The F-natural vibrato is played on the fifth hole or half of the fourth, the mordent on either the second or the fourth.

The F-sharp, or G-flat, vibrato is played in the same manner as F-natural. The mordent is played on the fourth hole, or on the first when it is preceded by an appoggiatura.

The G-natural vibrato is played on the fourth hole. The mordent is played on the second, or on the first when it is preceded by a whole-step appoggiatura.

The G-sharp, or A-flat, vibrato is played on half of the eighth hole. The mordent is played on the eighth hole itself, or on the sixth hole. In the latter case the third hole, and sometimes even the second, should be opened. When this manner is used, the hole should be restopped at the end. This method is not used for the other mordents.

The A-natural vibrato is played on the edge of the seventh hole. The mordent is played on the seventh hole itself. When it is preceded by a whole-step appoggiatura it is played on the fourth hole with the first and second open. Again, the hole must be stopped at the end.

The A-sharp, or B-flat, vibrato is played on the edge of the sixth hole, the mordent on the hole itself.

The B-natural vibrato is played on the edge of the fifth hole, the mordent on the hole itself.

The C-natural vibrato is played on the edge of the fifth or sixth holes, the mordent on either one of these two holes.

The C-sharp, or D-flat, vibrato is played on the edge of the sixth or fourth hole, the mordent on the fourth hole itself.

The D-natural vibrato is played on the edge of the fifth hole. The mordent is played on the fourth hole, or on the fifth when it is preceded by a half-step appoggiatura.

The D-sharp, or E-flat, vibrato is played on the edge of the fourth hole, the mordent on the hole itself.

The E-natural vibrato is played on half of the seventh hole. The mordent is played on the seventh hole itself, or on the fifth and sixth simultaneously when it is preceded by a whole-step appoggiatura.

The F-natural vibrato is played on the seventh hole, the mordent on the third.

The G-natural vibrato is played on the sixth hole, the mordent on the same hole.

End of the Treatise on the Recorder.

METHOD FOR OBOE

Method for Learning to Play the Oboe

The oboe has so much in common with the transverse flute, with regard to fingering, that it will be easy to play it by following the same rules. The difference between these two instruments, with regard to the fingering, appears only in a few notes. This difference is of such slight importance that the student will be perfectly well informed by reading the following instructions.

MANNER OF HOLDING THE OBOE

The oboe should be held approximately like the recorder, with this difference: it should be held twice as high. Consequently the head should be straight and the hands held high. The position of the hands is the same as that of the recorder, the right hand on the lower half of the instrument, the left hand on the upper half, etc.

THE EMBOUCHURE

With regard to the embouchure, the reed must be placed between the lips, squarely in the middle, approximately one quarter inch[16] into the mouth, so that about one eighth of an

---

16 These measurements are only approximate. The original French text reads: "Pour ce qui regarde l'Embouchure; il faut placer l'Anche entre les Levres, justement au milieu; on ne l'enfoncera dans la bouche que de l'épaisseur de deux ou trois lignes, ensorte qu'il y ait environ l'épaisseur d'une ligne & demie de distance, depuis les Levres jusqu'à la ligature de l'Anche...." See footnote 14, page 52.

71

inch remains between the lips and the binding of the reed. The reed should be placed in such a way that it can be pinched more or less, according to the need. The teeth should not touch the reed.

All the natural tones are produced in the manner shown in Plate 1 of the treatise on the transverse flute and explained in Chapter Three of the same treatise, with the exception of both high and low *C*, which are produced differently. The low *C* (note eleven) is produced by stopping the second hole[17] and leaving all the others open. The trill is played in the same manner as on the transverse flute, except that the trill is played on the third hole. (See the treatise on the transverse flute, Chapter Four, page 21.) The high *C* (note twenty-three) is produced by opening all the holes, or by opening only the first three and stopping the fourth, fifth and sixth.

There is also a lower *C* which is not shown on the chart because it is beyond the range of the transverse flute. It is produced by stopping all the holes and pressing the little finger on the large key which is at the lower end of the oboe. The trill is played on the same key. Note that tones above high *D* (note twenty-five) are almost never used. As the player ascends the scale it is important for him to blow gradually harder and to pinch the reed more with his lips.

All the sharps and flats are played according to the chart on the transverse flute. There are several exceptions which I shall explain.

Low *G*-flat (note fifty-three) is produced by opening the fifth hole entirely and the fourth only halfway, and by stopping all the others except that of the large key. The trill is played on the third hole. *F*-sharp (note five) is sometimes played in this manner and the trill on half of the fourth hole. *F*-sharp is,

---

17 The holes must be numbered as they were on the transverse flute. [This note is the only one by Hotteterre himself.]

nevertheless, usually played as it is on the transverse flute. High G-flat (note forty-one) is produced by stopping all the holes except the fourth and that of the large key. The trill is also played on the third hole. F-sharp (note seventeen) is produced in the same manner and is trilled by shaking on the fifth hole. F-sharp is also produced as it is on the transverse flute.

G-sharp, or A-flat (both high and low), is produced by opening half of the third hole, by stopping the first and second completely and by opening all the others. The G-sharp trill is played on half of the third hole. The A-flat trill is played on the second hole.

A-sharp, or B-flat (both high and low), is produced by stopping the first and third holes and leaving all the others open.

C-sharp, or D-flat (notes twelve and forty-six), is produced by opening the first hole and stopping all the others, including that of the large key. The C-sharp trill is played on the key with the little finger. The D-flat trill is played by stopping all the holes and trilling with the sixth finger. It can also be played as it is on the transverse flute. This semitone is also played an octave higher by blowing harder and by pinching the reed with the lips.

With regard to trills, tonguings, vibrati etc., the student should read the explanations given concerning these ornaments in the treatise on the transverse flute.

The End.